*Ralph
Waldo
Emerson.*

CHARACTER and Heroism.

CHARACTER and Heroism.

Ralph Waldo Emerson.

Fredonia Books
Amsterdam, The Netherlands

Character and Heroism

by
Ralph Waldo Emerson

ISBN: 1-58963-734-8

Reprinted from the 1900 edition

Fredonia Books
Amsterdam, the Netherlands
http://www.fredoniabooks.com

Character

Characters

Character

The sun set ; but set not his hope :
Stars rose ; his faith was earlier up :
Fixed on the enormous galaxy,
Deeper and older seemed his eye :
And matched his sufferance sublime
The taciturnity of time.
He spoke, and words more soft than rain
Brought the Age of Gold again :
His action won such reverence sweet,
As hid all measure of the feat.

Work of his hand
He nor commends nor grieves :
Pleads for itself the fact ;
As unrepenting Nature leaves
Her every act.

I HAVE read that those who listened to Lord Chatham felt that there was something finer in the man than anything which he said. It has been complained of our brilliant English historian of the French Revolution, that when he has told all his facts about Mirabeau, they do not justify his estimate of his genius. The Gracchi, Agis, Cleomenes, and others of Plutarch's heroes, do not in the record of facts equal their own fame. Sir Philip Sidney, the Earl of Essex, Sir Walter Raleigh, are men of great figure, and of few deeds. We cannot find the smallest part of the personal weight of Washington in the narrative of his exploits. The authority of the name of Schiller is too great for his books. This inequality of the reputa-

tion to the works or the anecdotes is
not accounted for by saying that the
reverberation is longer than the thun-
der-clap ; but somewhat resided in these
men which begot an expectation that
outran all their performance. The
largest part of their power was latent.
This is that which we call Character, —
a reserved force which acts directly by
presence, and without means. It is
conceived of as a certain undemon-
strable force, a Familiar or Genius, by
whose impulses the man is guided, but
whose counsels he cannot impart ;
which is company for him, so that
such men are often solitary, or if they
chance to be social, do not need society,
but can entertain themselves very well
alone. The purest literary talent
appears at one time great, at another

time small, but character is of a stellar
and undiminishable greatness. What
others effect by talent or by eloquence,
this man accomplishes by some mag-
netism. "Half his strength he put
not forth." His victories are by dem-
onstration of superiority, and not by
crossing of bayonets. He conquers,
because his arrival alters the face of
affairs. "O Iole! how did you know
that Hercules was a god?" "Because," answered Iole, "I was content
the moment my eyes fell on him. When
I beheld Theseus, I desired that I
might see him offer battle, or at least
guide his horses in the chariot-race;
but Hercules did not wait for a con-
test; he conquered whether he stood,
or walked, or sat, or whatever thing he
did." Man, ordinarily a pendant to

events, only half attached, and that awkwardly, to the world he lives in, in these examples appears to share the life of things, and to be an expression of the same laws which control the tides and the sun, numbers and quantities.

But to use a more modest illustration, and nearer home, I observe, that in our political elections, where this element, if it appears at all, can only occur in its coarsest form, we sufficiently understand its incomparable rate. The people know that they need in their representative much more than talent, namely, the power to make his talent trusted. They cannot come at their ends by sending to Congress a learned, acute, and fluent speaker, if he be not one who, before he was ap-

pointed by the people to represent
them, was appointed by Almighty God
to stand for a fact, — invincibly per-
suaded of that fact in himself, — so
that the most confident and the most
violent persons learn that here is resistance on which both impudence and
terror are wasted, namely, faith in a
fact. The men who carry their points
do not need to inquire of their constitu-
ents what they should say, but are
themselves the country which they
represent : nowhere are its emotions
or opinions so instant and true as in
them ; nowhere so pure from a selfish
infusion. The constituency at home
hearkens to their words, watches the
colour of their cheek, and therein, as in
a glass, dresses its own. Our public
assemblies are pretty good tests of

manly force. Our frank countrymen
of the West and South have a taste for
character, and like to know whether the
New Englander is a substantial man, or
whether the hand can pass through
him.

The same motive force appears in
trade. There are geniuses in trade, as
well as in war, or the state, or letters;
and the reason why this or that man is
fortunate, is not to be told. It lies in
the man: that is all anybody can tell
you about it. See him, and you will
know as easily why he succeeds as if
you saw Napoleon you would comprehend his fortune. In the new objects
we recognise the old game, the habit of
fronting the fact, and not dealing with
it at second hand, through the percep-
tions of somebody else. Nature seems

to authorise trade, as soon as you see
the natural merchant, who appears not
so much a private agent, as her factor
and Minister of Commerce. His natural probity combines with his insight
into the fabric of society to put him
above tricks, and he communicates to
all his own faith, that contracts are of
no private interpretation. The habit
of his mind is a reference to standards
of natural equity and public advantage;
and he inspires respect, and the wish to
deal with him, both for the quiet spirit
of honour which attends him, and for
the intellectual pastime which the spec-
tacle of so much ability affords. This
immensely stretched trade, which makes
the capes of the Southern Ocean his
wharves, and the Atlantic Sea his familiar port, centres in his brain only;

8

and nobody in the universe can make
his place good. In his parlour I see
very well that he has been at hard
work this morning, with that knitted
brow, and that settled humour, which
all his desire to be courteous cannot
shake off. I see plainly how many
firm acts have been done; how many
valiant *noes* have this day been spoken,
when others would have uttered ruin-
ous *yeas*. I see, with the pride of art,
and skill of masterly arithmetic and
power of remote combination, the
consciousness of being an agent and
playfellow of the original laws of the
world. He too believes that none can
supply him, and that a man must be
born to trade, or he cannot learn it.

This virtue draws the mind more,
when it appears in action to ends not

so mixed. It works with most energy
in the smallest companies and in private relations. In all cases, it is an
extraordinary and incomputable agent.
The excess of physical strength is
paralysed by it. Higher natures over-
power lower ones by affecting them
with a certain sleep. The faculties
are locked up, and offer no resistance.
Perhaps that is the universal law.
When the high cannot bring up the
low to itself, it benumbs it, as man
charms down the resistance of the
lower animals. Men exert on each
other a similar occult power. How
often has the influence of a true
master realised all the tales of magic!
A river of command seemed to run
down from his eyes into all those who
beheld him, a torrent of strong sad

light, like an Ohio or Danube, which pervaded them with his thoughts, and coloured all events with the hue of his mind. "What means did you employ?" was the question asked of the wife of Concini, in regard to her treatment of Mary of Medici; and the answer was, "Only that influence which every strong mind has over a weak one." Cannot Cæsar in irons, shuffle off the irons, and transfer them to the person of Hippo or Thraso the turnkey? Is an iron handcuff so immutable a bond? Suppose a slaver on the coast of Guinea should take on board a gang of negroes, which should contain persons of the stamp of Toussaint L'Ouverture: or, let us fancy, under these swarthy masks he has a gang of Washingtons in chains. When

they arrive at Cuba, will the relative
order of the ship's company be the
same ?   Is there nothing but rope and
iron ?   Is there no love, no reverence ?
Is there never a glimpse of right in a
poor slave-captain's mind ; and cannot
these be supposed available to break,
or elude, or in any manner overmatch
the tension of an inch or two of iron
ring ?

This is a natural power, the light
and heat, and all nature coöperates
with it. The reason why we feel
one man's presence, and do not feel another's is as simple as gravity. Truth
is the summit of being : justice is the
application of it to affairs. All individual natures stand in a scale, according to the purity of this element
in them. The will of the pure runs

down from them into other natures, as water runs down from a higher into a lower vessel. This natural force is no more to be withstood than any other natural force. We can drive a stone upward for a moment into the air, but it is yet true that all stones will for ever fall; and whatever instances can be quoted of unpunished thefts, or of a lie which somebody credited, justice must prevail, and it is the privilege of truth to make itself believed. Character is this moral order seen through the medium of an individual nature. An individual is an encloser. Time and space, liberty and necessity, truth and thought, are left at large no longer. Now, the universe is a close or pound. All things exist in the man tinged with the manners of his soul. With what quality is in him, he infuses all nature that he can reach; nor does he tend to lose himself in vastness, but, at how long a curve soever, all his regards return into his own good at last. He animates all he can, and he sees all he animates. He encloses the world, as the patriot does his country, as a material basis for his character, and a theatre for action. A healthy soul stands united with the Just and the True, as the magnet arranges itself with the pole, so that he stands to all beholders like a transparent object between them and the sun, and whoso journeys toward the sun, journeys toward that person. He is thus the medium of the highest influence to all who are not on the same level. Thus, men of character are the conscience of the society to which they belong.

The natural measure of this power is the resistance of circumstances. Impure men consider life as it is reflected in opinions, events, and persons. They cannot see the action until it is done. Yet its moral element preëxisted in the actor, and its quality as right or wrong it was easy to predict. Everything in nature is bipolar, or has a positive and negative pole. There is a male and a female, a spirit and a fact, a north and a south. Spirit is the positive, the event is the negative. Will is the north, action the south pole. Character may be ranked as having its natural place in the north. It shares the magnetic currents of the system. The feeble souls are drawn

to the south or negative pole. They
look at the profit or hurt of the action.
They never behold a principle until it
is lodged in a person. They do not
wish to be lovely, but to be loved.
The class of character like to hear of
their faults; the other class do not like
to hear of faults; they worship events;
secure to them a fact, a connection, a
certain chain of circumstances, and
they will ask no more. The hero
sees that the event is ancillary; it
must follow *him*. A given order of
events has no power to secure to him
the satisfaction which the imagination
attaches to it; the soul of goodness
escapes from any set of circumstances,
while prosperity belongs to a certain
mind, and will introduce that power
and victory which is its natural fruit,

into any order of events. No change
of circumstances can repair a defect of
character. We boast our emancipation
from many superstitions; but if we
have broken any idols, it is through a
transfer of the idolatry. What have I
gained, that I no longer immolate a
bull to Jove, or to Neptune, or a
mouse to Hecate; that I do not tremble
before the Eumenides, or the Catholic
Purgatory, or the Calvinistic Judg-
ment-day, — if I quake at opinion,
the public opinion, as we call it; or
at the threat of assault, or contumely,
or bad neighbours, or poverty, or muti-
lation, or at the rumour of revolution,
or of murder? If I quake, what
matters it what I quake at? Our
proper vice takes form in one or
another shape, according to the sex,

17

age, or temperament of the person,
and, if we are capable of fear, will
readily find terrors. The covetous-
ness, or the malignity which saddens
me, when I ascribe it to society, is
my own. I am always environed by
myself. On the other part, rectitude
is a perpetual victory, celebrated not
by cries of joy, but by serenity, which
is joy fixed or habitual. It is disgrace-
ful to fly to events for confirmation of
our truth and worth. The capitalist
does not run every hour to the broker,
to coin his advantages into current
money of the realm; he is satisfied to
read in the quotations of the market,
that his stocks have risen. The same
transport which the occurrence of the
best events in the best order would
occasion me, I must learn to taste

purer in the perception that my position is every hour meliorated, and does already command those events I desire. That exultation is only to be checked by the foresight of an order of things so excellent as to throw all our prosperities into the deepest shade.

The face which character wears to me is self-sufficingness. I revere the person who is riches; so that I cannot think of him as alone, or poor, or exiled, or unhappy, or a client, but as perpetual patron, benefactor, and beatified man. Character is centrality, the impossibility of being displaced or overset. A man should give us a sense of mass. Society is frivolous, and shreds its day into scraps, its conversation into ceremonies and escapes. But if I go to see an ingenious man,

I shall think myself poorly entertained
if he give me nimble pieces of benevolence and etiquette; rather he shall
stand stoutly in his place, and let me
apprehend, if it were only his resistance; know that I have encountered a
new and positive quality, — great re-
freshment for both of us. It is much,
that he does not accept the conven-
tional opinions and practices. That
non-conformity will remain a goad
and remembrancer, and every inquirer
will have to dispose of him, in the
first place. There is nothing real or
useful that is not a seat of war. Our
houses ring with laughter and personal
and critical gossip, but it helps little.
But the uncivil, the unavailable man,
who is a problem and a threat to society, whom it cannot let pass in si-

lence, but must either worship or hate,
— and to whom all parties feel related,
both the leaders of opinion, and the
obscure and eccentric, — he helps; he
puts America and Europe in the
wrong, and destroys the skepticism
which says, "man is a doll, let us
eat and drink, 'tis the best we can
do," by illuminating the untried and
unknown. Acquiescence in the es-
tablishment, and appeal to the public,
indicate infirm faith, heads which are
not clear, and which must see a house
built before they can comprehend the
plan of it. The wise man not only
leaves out of his thought the many,
but leaves out the few. Fountains,
fountains, the self-moved, the ab-
sorbed, the commander because he is
commanded, the assured, the primary,

— they are good; for these announce
the present pressure of supreme power.
Our action should rest mathemati-
cally on our substance. In nature
there are no false valuations. A pound
of water in the ocean-tempest has no
more gravity than in a midsummer
pond. All things work exactly according to their quality, and according to
their quantity; attempt nothing they
cannot do, except man only. He has
pretention; he wishes and attempts
things beyond his force. I read in
a book of English memoirs, "Mr.
Fox (afterward Lord Holland) said,
he must have the Treasury; he had
served up to it, and would have it."

Xenophon and his Ten Thousand
were quite equal to what they attempted
and did it; so equal that it was not

suspected to be a grand and inimitable exploit. Yet there stands that fact unrepeated, a high water mark in military history. Many have attempted it since and not been equal to it. It is only on reality, that any power of action can be based. No institution will be better than the institutor. I knew an aimable and accomplished person who undertook a practical reform, yet I was never able to find in him the enterprise of love he took in hand. He adopted it by ear and by the understanding from the books he had been reading. All his action was tentative, a piece of the city carried out into the fields, and was the city still and no new fact, and could not inspire enthusiasm. Had there been something latent in the man, a terrible undemonstrated genius agitating and embarrassing his demeanour, we had watched for its advent. It is not enough that the intellect should see the evils and their remedy. We shall still postpone our existence, nor take the ground to which we are entitled, while it is only a thought, and not a spirit that incites us. We have not yet served up to it.

These are properties of life, and another trait is the notice of incessant growth. Men should be intelligent and earnest. They must also make us feel that they have a controlling, happy future opening before them, which sheds a splendour on the passing hour. The hero is misconceived and misreported: he cannot therefore wait

to unravel any man's blunders; he is
again on his road, adding new powers
and honours to his domain, and new
claims on your heart, which will bank-
rupt you, if you have loitered about
the old things, and have not kept
your relation to him by adding to
your wealth.　New actions are the
only apologies and explanations of old
ones which the noble can bear to offer
or to receive.　If your friend has
displeased you, you shall not sit down
to consider it, for he has already lost
all memory of the passage, and has
doubled his power to serve you, and,
ere you can rise up again, will burden
you with blessings.

We have no pleasure in thinking
of a benevolence that is only measured
by its works. Love is inexhaustible,

and if its estate is wasted, its granary emptied, still cheers and enriches, and the man, though he sleep, seems to purify the air, and his house to adorn the landscape and strengthen the laws. People always recognise this difference. We know who is benevolent, by quite other means than the amount of subscription to soup-societies. It is only low merits that can be enumerated. Fear, when your friends say to you that you have done well, and say it through; but when they stand with uncertain timid looks of respect and half dislike, and must suspend their judgment for years to come, you may begin to hope. Those who live to the future must always appear selfish to those who live to the present. Therefore it was droll in the good

Character ✳

Riemer, who has written memoirs of Goethe, to make out a list of his donations and good deeds, as, so many hundred thalers given to Stilling, to Hegel, to Tischbein; a lucrative place found for Professor Voss, a post under the Grand Duke for Herder, a pension for Meyer, two professors recommended to foreign universities, etc., etc. The longest lists of specifications of benefit would look very short. A man is a poor creature, if he is to be measured so. For all these, of course, are exceptions; and the rule and hodiernal life of a good man is benefaction. The true charity of Goethe is to be inferred from the account he gave Doctor Eckermann, of the way in which he had spent his fortune. " Each bon-mot of mine

has cost a purse of gold. Half a
million of my own money, the fortune
I inherited, my salary, and the large
income derived from my writings for
fifty years back, have been expended to
instruct me in what I now know. I
have besides seen," etc.

I own it is but poor chat and gossip
to go to enumerate traits of this simple
and rapid power, and we are painting
the lightning in charcoal; but in these
long nights and vacations I like to
console myself so. Nothing but itself can copy it. A word warm from
the heart enriches me. I surrender
at discretion. How death-cold is literary genius before this fire of life!
These are the touches that reanimate
my heavy soul, and give it eyes to
pierce the dark of nature. I find,

where I thought myself poor, there was I most rich. Thence comes a new intellectual exaltation, to be again rebuked by some new exhibition of character. Strange alternation of attraction and repulsion! Character repudiates intellect, yet excites it; and character passes into thought, is published so, and then is ashamed before new flashes of moral worth.

Character is nature in the highest form. It is of no use to ape it, or to contend with it. Somewhat is possible of resistance, and of persistence, and of creation, to this power, which will foil all emulation.

This masterpiece is best where no hands but nature's have been laid on it. Care is taken that the greatly destined shall slip up into life in the shade, with no thousand-eyed Athens to watch and blazon every new thought, every blushing emotion of young genius. Two persons lately — very young children of the most high God — have given me occasion for thought. When I explored the source of their sanctity, and charm for the imagination, it seemed as if each answered, "From my non-conformity; I never listened to your people's law, or to what they call their gospel, and wasted my time. I was content with the simple rural poverty of my own; hence this sweetness; my work never reminds you of that, — is pure of that." And nature advertises me in such persons that, in democratic America, she will not be democratised. How cloistered and constitutionally sequestered from the market and from scandal! It was only this morning that I sent away some wild flowers of these wood-gods. They are a relief from literature, — these fresh draughts from the sources of thought and sentiment; as we read, in an age of polish and criticism, the first lines of written prose and verse of a nation. How captivating is their devotion to their favourite books, whether Æschylus, Dante, Shakespeare, or Scott, as feeling that they have a stake in that book; who touches that, touches them; and especially the total solitude of the critic, the Patmos of thought from which he writes, in unconsciousness of any eyes that shall ever read this writing. Could they dream on still, as angels, and not wake to comparisons

and to be flattered! Yet some natures
are too good to be spoiled by praise,
and wherever the vein of thought
reaches down into the profound, there
is no danger from vanity. Solemn
friends will warn them of the danger
of the head's being turned by the flour-
ish of trumpets, but they can afford
to smile. I remember the indignation
of an eloquent Methodist at the kind
admonitions of a Doctor of Divinity,
— "My friend, a man can neither
be praised nor insulted." But forgive
the counsels; they are very natural.
I remember the thought which occurred
to me when some ingenious and spiritual
foreigners came to America was, Have
you been victimised in being brought
hither? or, prior to that, answer me
this: "Are you victimisable?"

Character

As I have said, nature keeps these sovereignties in her own hands, and however pertly our sermons and disciplines would divide some share of credit, and teach that the laws fashion the citizen, she goes her own gait, and puts the wisest in the wrong. She makes very light of gospels and prophets, as one who has a great many more to produce, and no excess of time to spare on any one. There is a class of men, individuals of which appear at long intervals, so eminently endowed with insight and virtue, that they have been unanimously saluted as *divine*, and who seem to be an accumulation of that power we consider. Divine persons are character born, or, to borrow a phrase from Napoleon, they are victory organised. They are usually received with ill-will, because they are new, and because they set a bound to the exaggeration that has been made of the personality of the last divine person. Nature never rhymes her children, nor makes two men alike. When we see a great man, we fancy a resemblance to some historical person, and predict the sequel of his character and fortune, a result which he is sure to disappoint. None will ever solve the problem of his character according to our prejudice, but only in his own high unprecedented way. Character wants room ; must not be crowded on by persons, nor be judged from glimpses got in the press of affairs or on few occasions. It needs perspective, as a great building. It may not, probably does not, form relations rapidly; and we should not require rash explanation, either on the popular ethics, or on our own, of its action.

I look on Sculpture as history. I do not think the Apollo and the Jove impossible in flesh and blood. Every trait which the artist recorded in stone, he had seen in life, and better than his copy. We have seen many counterfeits, but we are born believers in great men. How easily we read in old books, when men were few, of the smallest action of the patriarchs. We require that a man should be so large and columnar in the landscape that it should deserve to be recorded that he arose and girded up his loins and departed to such a place. The most credible pictures are those of majestic men who prevailed at their entrance and convinced the senses, as happened to the Eastern magian who was sent to test the merits of Zertusht or Zoroaster. When the Yunani sage arrived at Balkh, the Persians tell us, Gushtasp appointed a day on which the Mobeds of every country should assemble, and a golden chair was placed for the Yunani sage. Then the beloved of Yezdam, the prophet Zertusht, advanced into the midst of the assembly. The Yunani sage, on seeing that chief, said, "This form and this gait cannot lie, and nothing but truth can proceed from them." Plato said, it was impossible not to believe in the children of the gods, "though they should speak without probable or necessary arguments." I should think myself very unhappy in my associates, if

36

Character ❊

I could not credit the best things in history. "John Bradshaw," says Milton, "appears like a counsel, from whom the fasces are not to depart with the year; so that not on the tribunal only, but throughout his life, you would regard him as sitting in judgment upon kings." I find it more credible since it is anterior information, that one man should *know heaven*, as the Chinese say, than that so many men should know the world. "The virtuous prince confronts the gods without any misgiving. He waits a hundred ages till a sage comes, and does not doubt. He who confronts the gods, without any misgiving, knows heaven; he who waits a hundred ages until a sage comes, without doubting, knows men. Hence the virtuous prince moves, and for ages shows empire the way." But there is no need to seek remote examples. He is a dull observer whose experience has not taught him the reality and force of magic, as well as of chemistry. The coldest precisian cannot go abroad without encountering inexplicable influences. One man fastens an eye on him, and the graves of the memory render up their dead; the secrets that make him wretched either to keep or to betray, must be yielded; another, and he cannot speak, and the bones of his body seem to lose their cartilages; the entrance of a friend adds grace, boldness, and eloquence to him; and there are persons, he cannot choose but remember, who gave a transcendent expansion to his thought, and kindled another life in his bosom.

38

Character ❋

What is so excellent as strict relations of amity, when they spring from this deep root? The sufficient reply to the skeptic, who doubts the power and the furniture of man, is in that possibility of joyful intercourse with persons which makes the faith and practice of all reasonable men. I know nothing which life has to offer so satisfying as the profound good understanding which can subsist, after much exchange of good offices, between two virtuous men, each of whom is sure of himself, and sure of his friend. It is a happiness which postpones all other gratifications, and makes politics, and commerce, and churches cheap. For when men shall meet as they ought, each a benefactor, a shower of stars clothed with thoughts, with deeds, with

accomplishments, it should be the festival of nature which all things announce.
Of such friendship, love in the sexes is
the first symbol, as all other things are
symbols of love. Those relations to
the best men which, at one time, we
reckoned the romances of youth, become, in the progress of the character,
the most solid enjoyment.

If it were possible to live in right
relations with men ! — if we could
abstain from asking anything of them,
from asking their praise, or help, or
pity, and content us with compelling
them through the virtue of the eldest
laws ! Could we not deal with a few
persons — with one person — after the
unwritten statutes, and make an experi-
ment of their efficacy ? Could we not
pay our friend the compliment of truth,

of silence, of forebearing? Need we
be so eager to seek him? If we
are related, we shall meet. It was a
tradition of the ancient world that no
metamorphosis could hide a god from
a god; and there is a Greek verse which
runs,

"The Gods are to each other not unknown."

Friends also follow the laws of divine
necessity; they gravitate to each other,
and cannot otherwise:

"When each the other shall avoid,
    Shall each by each be most enjoyed."

Their relation is not made, but
allowed. The gods must seat themselves without seneschal in our Olympus, and as they can install themselves
by seniority divine. Society is spoiled,

if pains are taken, if the associates are brought a mile to meet. And if it be not society, it is a mischievous, low, degrading jangle, though made up of the best. All the greatness of each is kept back, and every foible in painful activity, as if the Olympians should meet to exchange snuff-boxes.

Life goes headlong. We chase some flying scheme, or we are hunted by some fear or command behind us. But if suddenly we encounter a friend, we pause; our heat and hurry look foolish enough; now pause, now possession is required, and the power to swell the moment from the resources of the heart. The moment is all, in all noble relations.

A divine person is the prophecy of

the mind ; a friend is the hope of the
heart. Our beatitude waits for the
fulfilment of these two in one. The
ages are opening this moral force. All
force is the shadow or symbol of that.
Poetry is joyful and strong, as it draws
its inspiration thence. Men write their
names on the world, as they are filled
with this. History has been mean ;
our nations have been mobs ; we have
never seen a man : that divine form we
do not yet know, but only the dream
and prophecy of such : we do not know
the majestic manners which belong to
him, which appease and exalt the be-
holder. We shall one day see that the
most private is the most public energy,
that quality atones for quantity, and
grandeur of character acts in the dark,
and succours them who never saw it.

What greatness has yet appeared is be-
ginnings and encouragements to us in
this direction. The history of those
gods and saints which the world has
written, and then worshipped, are docu-
ments of character. The ages have
exulted in the manners of a youth who
owed nothing to fortune, and who was
hanged at the Tyburn of his nation,
who, by the pure quality of his nature,
shed an epic splendour around the facts
of his death, which has transfigured
every particular into an universal symbol for the eyes of mankind. This
great defeat is hitherto our highest fact.
But the mind requires a victory to the
senses, a force of character which will
convert judge, jury, soldier, and king;
which will rule animal and mineral
virtues, and blend with the courses of

sap, of rivers, of winds, of stars, and of moral agents.

If we cannot attain at a bound to these grandeurs, at least let us do them homage. In society, high advantages are set down to the possessor as disadvantages. It requires the more wariness in our private estimates. I do not forgive in my friends the failure to know a fine character and to entertain it with thankful hospitality. When, at last, that which we have always longed for is arrived, and shines on us with glad rays out of that far celestial land, then to be coarse, then to be critical, and treat such a visitant with the jabber and suspicion of the streets, argues a vulgarity that seems to shut the doors of heaven. This is confusion, this the right insanity, when the

soul no longer knows its own, nor
where its allegiance, its religion, are
due. Is there any religion but this to
know, that wherever in the wide desert
of being the holy sentiment we cherish
has opened into a flower it blooms for
me? If none sees it, I see it; I am
aware, if I alone, of the greatness of
the fact. While it blooms I will keep
sabbath or holy time and suspend my
gloom and my folly and jokes. Nature
is indulged by the presence of this
guest. There are many eyes that can
detect and honour the prudent and
household virtues; there are many that
can discern Genius on his starry track,
though the mob is incapable; but
when that love which is all-suffering,
all-abstaining, all-aspiring, which has
vowed to itself that it will be a wretch

46

and also a fool in this world sooner
than soil its white hands by any com-
pliances, comes into our streets and
houses, — only the pure and aspiring
can know its face, and the only compliment they can pay it is to own it.

Heroism

Heroism

"Paradise is under the shadow of swords."
— *Mahomet.*

IN the elder English dramatists, and mainly in the plays of Beaumont and Fletcher, there is a constant recognition of gentility, as if a noble behaviour were as easily marked in the society of their age, as colour is in our American population. When any Rodrigo, Pedro, or Valerio enters, though he be a stranger, the duke or governor exclaims, This is a gentleman, — and proffers civilities without end; but all the rest are slag and refuse. In har-

mony with this delight in personal advantages, there is in their plays a
certain heroic cast of character and
dialogue — as in Bonduca, Sophocles,
the Mad Lover, the Double Marriage
— wherein the speaker is so earnest
and cordial, and on such deep grounds
of character, that the dialogue, on the
slightest additional incident in the plot,
rises naturally into poetry. Among
many texts, take the following. The
Roman Martius has conquered Athens,
— all but the invincible spirits of
Sophocles, the duke of Athens, and
Dorigen, his wife. The beauty of
the latter inflames Martius, and he
seeks to save her husband; but Sophocles will not ask his life, although
assured that a word will save him,
and the execution of both proceeds.

Heroism ❁

"*Valerius.* Bid thy wife farewell.

  Soph. No, I will take no leave. My
     Dorigen,

Yonder, above, 'bout Ariadne's crown,

My spirit shall hover for thee. Prithee, haste.

  Dor. Stay, Sophocles — with this, tie up
     my sight ;

Let not soft nature so transformed be,

And lose her gentler sexed humanity,

To make me see my lord bleed. So, 'tis
     well ;

Never one object underneath the sun

Will I behold before my Sophocles :

Farewell ; now teach the Romans how to
     die.

  Mar. Dost know what 'tis to die ?

  Soph. Thou dost not, Martius,

And therefore, not what 'tis to live ; to die

Is to begin to live. It is to end

An old, stale, weary work, and to commence

A newer, and a better. 'Tis to leave

Deceitful knaves for the society
Of gods and goodness. Thou, thyself,
    must part
At last, from all thy garlands, pleasures,
    triumphs,
And prove thy fortitude what then 'twill do.
    Val.   But art not grieved nor vexed to
       leave thy life thus?
    Soph.   Why should I grieve or vex for
       being sent
To them I ever loved best? Now, I'll kneel,
But with my back toward thee; 'tis the last
    duty
This trunk can do the gods.
    Mar.   Strike, strike, Valerius,
Or Martius' heart will leap out at his mouth:
This is a man, a woman! Kiss thy lord,
And live with all the freedom you were wont.
O love! thou doubly hast afflicted me
With virtue and with beauty.   Treacherous
    heart,

54

Heroism ✹

My hand shall cast the quick into my urn,
Ere thou transgress this knot of piety.
   Val.   What ails my brother ?
   Soph.   Martius, oh Martius,
Thou now hast found a way to conquer me.
   Dor.   O star of Rome ! what gratitude
    can speak
Fit words to follow such a deed as this ?
   Mar.   This admirable duke, Valerius,
With his disdain of fortune and of death,
Captived himself, has captived me,
And though my arm hath ta'en his body here,
His soul hath subjugated Martius' soul.
By Romulus, he is all soul, I think ;
He hath no flesh, and spirit cannot be gyved ;
Then we have vanquished nothing ; he is free,
And Martius walks now in captivity."

I do not readily remember any poem,
play, sermon, novel, or oration, that
our press vents in the last few years,
which goes to the same tune. We

have a great many flutes and flageolets, but not often the sound of any fife. Yet, Wordsworth's Laodamia, and the ode of " Dion," and some sonnets, have a certain noble music; and Scott will sometimes draw a stroke like the portrait of Lord Evandale, given by Balfour of Burley. Thomas Carlyle, with his natural taste for what is manly and daring in character, has suffered no heroic trait in his favourites to drop from his biographical and historical pictures. Earlier, Robert Burns has given us a song or two. In the Harleian Miscellanies, there is an account of the battle of Lutzen, which deserves to be read. And Simon Ockley's History of the Saracens recounts the prodigies of individual valour with admiration, all the more evident on the part of the narrator, that he seems to think that his place in Christian Oxford requires of him some proper protestations of abhorrence. But if we explore the literature of Heroism, we shall quickly come to Plutarch, who is its Doctor and historian. To him we owe the Brasidas, the Dion, the Epaminondas, the Scipio of old, and I must think we are more deeply indebted to him than to all the ancient writers. Each of his " Lives " is a refutation to the despondency and cowardice of our religious and political theorists. A wild courage, a stoicism not of the schools, but of the blood, shines in every anecdote, and has given that book its immense fame.

We need books of this tart cathartic virtue, more than books of political science, or of private economy. Life is a festival only to the wise. Seen from the nook and chimney-side of prudence, it wears a ragged and dangerous front. The violations of the laws of nature by our predecessors and our contemporaries, are punished in us also. The disease and deformity around us certify the infraction of natural, intellectual, and moral laws, and often violation on violation to breed such compound misery. A lockjaw, that bends a man's head back to his heels, hydrophobia, that makes him bark at his wife and babes, insanity, that makes him eat grass; war, plague, cholera, famine, indicate a certain ferocity in nature, which, as it had its inlet by human crime, must have its outlet by human suffering. Unhappily, almost

no man exists who has not in his own
person become, to some amount, a
stockholder in the sin, and so made
himself liable to a share in the expia-
tion.

Our culture, therefore, must not
omit the arming of the man. Let him
hear in season that he is born into the
state of war, and that the common-
wealth and his own well-being require
that he should not go dancing in the
weeds of peace, but warned, self-col-
lected, and neither defying nor dread-
ing the thunder, let him take both
reputation and life in his hand, and
with perfect urbanity, dare the gibbet
and the mob by the absolute truth of
his speech and the rectitude of his
behaviour.

Toward all this external evil the

man within the breast assumes a war-
like attitude, and affirms his ability to
cope single-handed with the infinite
army of enemies. To this military
attitude of the soul we give the name
of Heroism. Its rudest form is the
contempt for safety and ease which
makes the attractiveness of war. It is
a self-trust which slights the restraints
of prudence in the plenitude of its
energy and power to repair the harms
it may suffer. The hero is a mind of
such balance that no disturbances can
shake his will, but pleasantly, and, as
it were, merrily, he advances to his
own music, alike in frightful alarms,
and in the tipsy mirth of universal
dissoluteness. There is somewhat not
philosophical in heroism; there is somewhat not holy in it; it seems not to

know that other souls are of one tex-
ture with it; it hath pride; it is the
extreme of individual nature. Never-
theless, we must profoundly revere it.
There is somewhat in great actions
which does not allow us to go behind them. Heroism feels and never
reasons, and therefore is always right,
and although a different breeding, different religion, and greater intellectual
activity would have modified, or even
reversed the particular action, yet for
the hero, that thing he does is the
highest deed, and is not open to the
censure of philosophers or divines. It
is the avowal of the unschooled man,
that he finds a quality in him that is
negligent of expense, of health, of life,
of danger, of hatred, of reproach, and
that he knows that his will is higher

and more excellent than all actual and all possible antagonists.

Heroism works in contradiction to the voice of mankind, and in contradiction, for a time, to the voice of the great and good. Heroism is an obedience to a secret impulse of an individual's character. Now to no other man can its wisdom appear as it does to him, for every man must be supposed to see a little farther on his own proper path, than any one else. Therefore, just and wise men take umbrage at his act, until after some little time be past: then, they see it to be in unison with their acts. All prudent men see that the action is clean contrary to a sensual prosperity; for every heroic act measures itself by its contempt of some external good. But it finds its own success at last, and then the prudent also extol.

Self-trust is the essence of heroism. It is the state of the soul at war, and its ultimate objects are the last defiance of falsehood and wrong, and the power to bear all that can be inflicted by evil agents. It speaks the truth, and it is just. It is generous, hospitable, temperate, scornful of petty calculations, and scornful of being scorned. It persists; it is of an undaunted boldness, and of a fortitude not to be wearied out. Its jest is the littleness of common life. That false prudence which dotes on health and wealth, is the foil, the butt, and merriment of heroism. Heroism, like Plotinus, is almost ashamed of its body. What shall it say, then, to the sugar-plums, and cats'-cradles, to the toilet, compliments, quarrels, cards, and custard, which rack the wit of all human society? What joys has kind nature provided for us dear creatures! There seems to be no interval between greatness and meanness. When the spirit is not master of the world, then is it dupe. Yet the little man takes the great hoax so innocently, works in it so headlong and believing, is born red, and dies gray, arranging his toilet, attending on his own health, laying traps for sweet food and strong wine, setting his heart on a horse or a rifle, made happy with a little gossip, or a little praise, that the great soul cannot choose but laugh at such earnest nonsense. " Indeed, these humble considerations make me out of love with greatness. What a disgrace is it to me to take note how many pairs of silk stockings thou hast, namely, these and those that were the peach-coloured ones or to bear the inventory of thy shirts, as one for superfluity, and one other for use."

Citizens, thinking after the laws of arithmetic, consider the inconvenience of receiving strangers at their fireside, reckon narrowly the loss of time and the unusual display : the soul of a better quality thrusts back the unreasonable economy into the vaults of life, and says, I will obey the God, and the sacrifice and the fire he will provide. Ibn Hankal, the Arabian geographer, describes a heroic extreme in the hospitality of Sogd, in Bokhara. "When I was in Sogd I saw a great building, like a palace, the gates of which were open and fixed back to the wall with large nails. I asked the reason, and was told that the house had not been shut, night or day, for a hundred years. Strangers may present themselves at any hour, and in whatever number; the master has amply provided for the reception of the men and their animals, and is never happier than when they tarry for some time. Nothing of the kind have I seen in any other country." The magnanimous know very well that they who give time, or money, or shelter, to the stranger, — so it be done for love, and not for ostentation, — do, as it were, put God under obligation to them, so perfect are the compensations of the universe. In some way the time they seem to lose is redeemed, and the pains they seem to

take remunerate themselves. These
men fan the flame of human love and
raise the standard of civil virtue among
mankind. But hospitality must be for
service, and not for show, or it pulls
down the host. The brave soul rates
itself too high to value itself by the
splendour of its table and draperies. It
gives what it hath, and all it hath, but
its own majesty can lend a better grace
to bannocks and fair water, than belong to city feasts.

The temperance of the hero proceeds from the same wish to do no
dishonour to the worthiness he has.
But he loves it for its elegancy, not
for its austerity. It seems not worth
his while to be solemn, and denounce
with bitterness flesh-eating, or wine-
drinking, the use of tobacco, or opium,

or tea, or silk, or gold. A great man
scarcely knows how he dines, how he
dresses, but without railing or preci-
sion, his living is natural and poetic.
John Eliot, the Indian Apostle, drank
water, and said of wine, " It is a noble, generous liquor, and we should be
humbly thankful for it. But, as I
remember, water was made before it."
Better still, is the temperance of King
David, who poured out on the ground
unto the Lord the water which three
of his warriors had brought him to
drink, at the peril of their lives.

It is told of Brutus, that when he
fell on his sword, after the battle of
Philippi, he quoted a line of Euripi-
des, " O virtue, I have followed thee
through life, and I find thee at last but
a shade." I doubt not the hero is

slandered by this report. The heroic
soul does not sell its justice and its
nobleness. It does not ask to dine
nicely, and to sleep warm. The essence of greatness is the perception
that virtue is enough. Poverty is its
ornament. Plenty, it does not need,
and can very well abide its loss.

But that which takes my fancy
most, in the heroic class, is the good
humour and hilarity they exhibit. It
is a height to which common duty can
very well attain, to suffer and to dare
with solemnity. But these rare souls
set opinion, success, and life at so
cheap a rate, that they will not soothe
their enemies by petitions, or the show
of sorrow, but wear their own habitual
greatness. Scipio, charged with pecu-
lation, refuses to do himself so great a

disgrace as to wait for justification, though he had the scroll of his accounts in his hands, but tears it to pieces before the tribunes. Socrates's condemnation of himself to be maintained in all honour in the Prytaneum, during his life, and Sir Thomas More's playfulness at the scaffold, are of the same strain. In Beaumont and Fletcher's "Sea Voyage," Juletta tells the stout captain and his company,

"*Jul.* Why, slaves, 'tis in our power to hang ye.
  Master.   Very likely,
'Tis in our powers, then, to be hanged, and scorn ye."

These replies are sound and whole. Sport is the bloom and glow of a perfect health. The great will not

condescend to take anything seriously;
all must be as gay as the song of a
canary, though it were the building of
cities or the eradication of old and
foolish churches and nations, which
have cumbered the earth long thou-
sands of years. Simple hearts put all
the history and customs of this world
behind them, and play their own play
in innocent defiance of the Blue-Laws
of the world; and such would appear,
could we see the human race assembled
in vision, like little children frolicking
together, though, to the eyes of mankind at large, they wear a stately and
solemn garb of works and influences.

The interest these fine stories have
for us, the power of a romance over
the boy who grasps the forbidden book
under his bench at school, our delight in

the hero, is the main fact to our pur-
pose. All these great and transcendent
properties are ours. If we dilate in be-
holding the Greek energy, the Roman
pride, it is that we are already domesti-
cating the same sentiment. Let us
find room for this great guest in our
small houses. The first step of worthiness will be to disabuse us of our
superstitious associations with places
and times, with number and size.
Why should these words, Athenian,
Roman, Asia, and England, so tingle
in the ear? Let us feel that where the
heart is, there the muses, there the gods
so sojourn, and not in any geography
of fame. Massachusetts, Connecticut
River, and Boston Bay, you think paltry
places, and the ear loves names of
foreign and classic topography. But

here we are; that is a great fact, and,
if we will tarry a little, we may come
to learn that here is best. See to it
only that thyself is here; and art and
nature, hope and dread, friends, angels
and the Supreme Being, shall not be
absent from the chamber where thou
sittest. Epaminondas, brave and affec-
tionate, does not seem to us to need
Olympus to die upon, nor the Syrian
sunshine. He lies very well where he
is. The Jerseys were handsome ground
enough for Washington to tread, and
London streets for the feet of Milton.
A great man illustrates his place, makes
his climate genial in the imagination of
men, and its air the beloved element
of all delicate spirits. That country
is the fairest, which is inhabited by the
noblest minds. The pictures which

73

fill the imagination in reading the actions of Pericles, Xenophon, Columbus, Bayard, Sidney, Hampden, teach us how needlessly mean our life is, that we, by the depth of our living, should deck it with more than regal or national splendour, and act on principles that should interest man and nature in the length of our days.

We have seen or heard of many extraordinary young men, who never ripened, or whose performance in actual life was not extraordinary. When we see their air and mien, when we hear them speak of society, of books, of religion, we admire their superiority — they seem to throw contempt on the whole state of the world; theirs is the tone of a youthful giant, who is sent to work revolutions. But they enter

an active profession, and the forming
Colossus shrinks to the common size
of man. The magic they used was the
ideal tendencies, which always make
the actual ridiculous; but the tough
world had its revenge the moment they
put their horses of the sun to plough in
its furrow. They found no example
and no companion, and their heart
fainted. What then? The lesson
they gave in their first aspirations, is
yet true, and a better valour, and a
purer truth, shall one day execute their
will, and put the world to shame. Or
why should a woman liken herself to
any historical woman, and think, because Sappho, or Sévigné, or De Staël,
or the cloistered souls who have had
genius and cultivation, do not satisfy
the imagination, and the serene Themis,

none can, — certainly not she. Why
not? She has a new and unattempted
problem to solve, perchance that of the
happiest nature that ever bloomed.
Let the maiden, with erect soul, walk
serenely on her way, accept the hint
of each new experience, try, in turn,
all the gifts God offers her, that she
may learn the power and the charm,
that like a new dawn radiating out of
the deep of space, her new-born being
is. The fair girl, who repels interfer-
ence by a decided and proud choice of
influences, so careless of pleasing, so
wilful and lofty, inspires every be-
holder with somewhat of her own
nobleness. The silent heart encour-
ages her; O friend, never strike sail to
a fear. Come into port greatly, or sail
with God the seas. Not in vain you

live, for every passing eye is cheered
and refined by the vision.

The characteristic of a genuine heroism is its persistency. All men have
wandering impulses, fits and starts of
generosity. But when you have re-
solved to be great, abide by yourself,
and do not weakly try to reconcile
yourself with the world. The heroic
cannot be the common, nor the common heroic. Yet we have the weakness
to expect the sympathy of people in
those actions whose excellence is that
they outrun sympathy, and appeal to a
tardy justice. If you would serve your
brother, because it is fit for you to
serve him, do not take back your words
when you find that prudent people do
not commend you. Be true to your
own act, and congratulate yourself if

you have done something strange and extravagant, and broken the monotony of a decorous age. It was a high counsel that I once heard given to a young person: "Always do what you are afraid to do." A simple manly character need never make an apology, but should regard its past action with the calmness of Phocion, when he admitted that the event of the battle was happy, yet did not regret his dissuasion from the battle.

There is no weakness or exposure for which we cannot find consolation in the thought — this is a part of my constitution, part of my relation and office to my fellow creature. Has nature convenanted with me, that I should never appear to disadvantage, never make a ridiculous figure? Let

us be generous of our dignity as well
as of our money. Greatness once and
for ever has done with opinion. We
tell our charities, not because we wish
to be praised for them, not because
we think they have great merit, but
for our justification. It is a capital
blunder; as you discover when another
man recites his charities.

To speak the truth, even with some
austerity, to live with some rigour
of temperance, or some extremes of
generosity, seems to be an asceticism
which common good nature would
appoint to those who are at ease and in
plenty, in sign that they feel a brother-
hood with the great multitude of suffering men. And not only need we
breathe and exercise the soul by assum-
ing the penalties of abstinence, of debt,

of solitude, of unpopularity, but it be-
hooves the wise man to look with a
bold eye into those rarer dangers which
sometimes invade men, and to familiar-
ise himself with disgusting forms of
disease, with sounds of execration, and
the vision of violent death.

Times of heroism are generally times
of terror, but the day never shines, in
which this element may not work.
The circumstances of man, we say,
are historically somewhat better in this
country, and at this hour, than perhaps
ever before. More freedom exists for
culture. It will not now run against
an axe, at the first step out of the
beaten track of opinion. But whoso
is heroic will always find crises to try
his edge. Human virtue demands her
champions and martyrs, and the trial

of persecution always proceeds. It is but the other day that the brave Lovejoy gave his breast to the bullets of a mob for the rights of free speech and opinion, and died when it was better not to live.

I see not any road of perfect peace, which a man can walk, but to take counsel of his own bosom. Let him quit too much association, let him go home much, and establish himself in those courses he approves. The unremitting retention of simple and high sentiments in obscure duties is hardening the character to that temper which will work with honour, if need be, in the tumult, or on the scaffold. Whatever outrages have happened to men may befall a man again; and very easily in a republic, if there appear any signs of a decay of religion. Coarse slander, fire, tar and feathers, and the gibbet, the youth may freely bring home to his mind, and with what sweetness of temper he can, and inquire how fast he can fix his sense of duty, braving such penalties, whenever it may please the next newspaper, and a sufficient number of his neighbours, to pronounce his opinions incendiary.

It may calm the apprehension of calamity, in the most susceptible heart, to see how quick a bound nature has set to the utmost infliction of malice. We rapidly approach a brink over which no enemy can follow us.

> " Let them rave :
> Thou art quiet in thy grave. "

In the gloom of our ignorance of what shall be, in the hour when we are deaf

to the higher voices, who does not envy
them who have seen safely to an end
their manful endeavour? Who that
sees the meanness of our politics, but
inly congratulates Washington, that he
is long already wrapped in his shroud,
and for ever safe ; that he was laid sweet
in his grave, the hope of humanity not
yet subjugated in him ? Who does not
sometimes envy the good and brave,
who are no more to suffer from the
tumults of the natural world, and await
with curious complacency the speedy
term of his own conversation with
finite nature ? And yet the love that
will be annihilated sooner than treacherous has already made death impossible,
and affirms itself no mortal, but a
native of the deeps of absolute and
inextinguishable being.

HELPING YOUR CHILDREN CHOOSE THEIR HEROES THROUGH READING

by

Adam Starchild

Children today are starved for the image of real heroes. Celebrities are not the same thing as heroes. Heroes existed way before celebrities ever did, even though celebrities now outshine heroes in children's consciousness.

Worshiping celebrities leaves children with a distinctly empty feeling -- it doesn't teach that they'll have to make sacrifices if they want to achieve anything worthwhile. No-talents become celebrities all the time. The result is that people don't

85

seem to care about achievement or talent -- fame is the only objective.

What is a hero? Despite immense differences in cultures, heroes around the world generally share a number of traits that instruct and inspire people. A hero does something worth talking about, but a hero goes beyond mere fame or celebrity. The hero lives a life worthy of imitation. If they serve only their own fame, they may be celebrities but not heroes. Heroes are catalysts for change. They create new possibilities. They have a vision, and the skill and charm to implement their vision.

Heroes may also be fictional. Children may identify with a character because of the values projected. People tend to grow to be like the people that they admire, but if a child never has any heroes what images will he copy? Adults need heroes too, but the need is even more urgent for children because they don't know how to think abstractly. But they can imagine what their hero would do in the circumstances, and it gives them a useful reference point to build abstract thinking skills.

Good reading selections can help your children find their own heroes -- to provide the emotional experience of admiring a figure they can look up to. Through the wide variety of reading experiences and choices of heroes, your children will find those models that best suit them.

It is important that children become familiar with worthy examples -- both real and fictional -- that they can emulate.

This does not mean that everything they read needs to be populated with heroes. Children will turn away from fictional villains they don't like. It is important to avoid children's stories in which the hero commits and gets away with evil actions. Don't assume that because a story is traditional it is automatically the literature you want your child to read. It is easy to think "that's o.k., it's a traditional children's story and I know it isn't dirty" without giving a moment's thought to the other messages that the story might be subconsciously conveying to your child.

Goldilocks and the Three Bears is certainly a traditional story, and most parents buy the book almost automatically, without a thought to the message. Goldilocks is lost and frightened, goes to a house and knocks, but no one is home. But that doesn't justify the crimes that follow. Yes, crimes! Breaking and entering, petty vandalism and theft -- even the nerve to go to sleep in a bed which doesn't belong to her either.

Is this really what you intended to teach your child -- that if you get lost it is alright to break into anybody's house and use their property? The story may be traditional, but these aren't the values you want to be teaching. It is so easy to assume that a well known book is okay, and select it for your child without even being aware of the subtle messages that it conveys -- messages that may be having far more influence on your child than you realize. After all, aren't you the one that told your child that this was a good book -- or read the story aloud? As your child is exposed to these traditional stories, you will want to take the time to explain the lessons in them. Without this guidance you may be unknowingly confusing the child. A child can also become confused when the villains in the story are likeable people who do evil.

Visible heroes today may be a bit harder to find and less dramatic, which is all the more reason to help your children start with the clear cut fictional heroes and then gradually transfer those learned ideals to the real world around them. There is no better place for a child to start than well-selected stories and novels where the hero has ability and integrity -- somebody who accomplishes an important, positive job.

All children start life with the same empty brain cells. What the adults around them put into those minds determines the resulting personalities. Stories -- whether heard or read -- are some of the most fundamental influences on a child.

One writer whose books are highly suitable for all ages is Robert Heinlein. He uses a science fiction format to deliver important messages, and it is often easier for a child to receive and understand the message when the setting is entirely unfamiliar and the characters and events can therefore be seen more clearly. For an older child you might want to start with *The Past Through Tomorrow*, a collection of his shorter stories. This lets the child break the reading into distinct units. For younger children look for *Podkayne of Mars*, *Between Planets*, or *Have Spacesuit, Will Travel*.

Afterword

If your child likes westerns, try some of the books by Louis L'Amour.

For preschoolers, any Dr. Seuss books. They may not be obvious as sources of heroes from an adult viewpoint, but from a small child's viewpoint they have characters that are easy to remember.

For the whole family, try *The Fire Hunter* by Jim Kjelgaard or *Girl Who Owned a City* by O. T. Nelson. And Heinlein's *The Rolling Stones* or *Farmer in the Sky*. Both are strong family books about future pioneers who have to solve problems for themselves. These heroes had to make themselves intelligent and capable to make a new, better life for themselves.

Don't dismiss heroes just because they are fictional. The power of creative imagination is one that is critically important to develop in children. When they learn to imagine with confidence and pleasure things they can't actually see, it is the first

step towards conceptualization and abstract
thinking -- important skills for handling adult
challenges.

Afterword

About the Author

Over the past 25 years, Adam Starchild has been the author of several dozen books, and hundreds of magazine articles, primarily on business and finance. His articles have appeared in a wide range of publications around the world.

Now semi-retired, he was the president of an international consulting group specializing in banking, finance and the development of new businesses, and director of a trust company.

Although this formidable testimony to expertise in his field, plus his current preoccupation with other books-in-progress, would not seem to leave time for a well-rounded existence, Starchild has won two Presidential Sports Awards and written several cookbooks, and is currently involved in a number of personal charitable projects.

His website is at http://www.adamstarchild.com/

www.ingramcontent.com/pod-product-compliance
Lightning Source LLC
Chambersburg PA
CBHW011406010726
47495CB00009B/2801